Black's Sketchbooks

1 London
2 Edinburgh
3 Cambridge
4 Stratford on Avon
5 Bath and Wells
6 Canterbury
7 Brighton & Environs
8 Chester
9 Durham
10 Oxford
11 The English Lakes
12 The Thames

PUBLISHED BY
A. & C. BLACK · SOHO SQUARE · LONDON W.

CHESTER

A SKETCH-BOOK BY

Joseph Pike

A & C. BLACK LTD. LONDON. W. 1.

LIST OF SKETCHES BY
JOSEPH PIKE

FOREGATE STREET

THE CATHEDRAL FROM THE CITY WALLS

THE CATHEDRAL CLOISTERS

Joseph Pike

THE TOWN HALL AND NORTHGATE STREET

THE CANAL AND BRIDGE OF SIGHS

THE WATER TOWER

THE OLD DEE BRIDGE

Joseph Pike

SALMON FISHING BOATS ON THE RIVER DEE Joseph Pike

CHESTER CASTLE

Joseph Pennell

THE BEAR AND BILLET

Joseph Pike

OLD HOUSE IN LOWER BRIDGE STREET

Joseph Pike

THE FALCON INN

THE LADY'S BOWER. LECHE HOUSE

THE ROWS AT BISHOP LLOYD'S PALACE

Joseph Pike

THE ROWS · WATERGATE STREET

OLD STANLEY PALACE

THE FIREPLACE AT STANLEY PALACE

Joseph Pike

ANTIQUES
OLD HOUSES
WATERGATE STREET.
"UNCLE TOM'S CABIN"
Joseph Pike

GODS·PROVIDENCE·IS·MINE·INHERITANCE
R. DAVIES & Co
THE OLD CRYPT
PROVIDENCE HOUSE

HOUSES IN BRIDGE STREET

THE CROSS

Joseph Pike
SOUTH AISLE
ST JOHN'S CHURCH

St JOHN'S RUINS